Catch Your Balance And Run

Proven Life Management Strategies To Assist You In Today's Fast-Paced World

MICHAEL SCOTT

Catch Your Balance And Run!

Catch Your Balance And Run

by

MICHAEL SCOTT

Published by:
EMPOWERMENT UNLIMITED INC.

May 1998

Copyright © 1998 by Empowerment Unlimited Inc.

All rights reserved.

Printed in the United States of America.

Cover photography by McGleam Photography, Lisle, Illinois
Cover art and page layout by Ad Graphics, Tulsa, Oklahoma

ISBN: 0-9661045-7-9

THANK YOU
● ● ● ● ● ●

Special thanks to Carolyn Neal, who handled the word processing and editing of this book, and Mershon Shrigley of Shrigley and Associates for your comprehensive editorial review. Kudos to Joy Loverde, Therese Kienast, Teresa Halgren and JoAnna Slan for your brutally honest advice and comments regarding the manuscript.

To my wife Angie and daughter Crystal, thank you for being there when I needed you most. I love you!

SPECIAL ACKNOWLEDGMENT
• • • • • • •

Special thanks to David Bell of Incredible Speakers Bureau in Orlando, Florida, for his generous investment in support of this book.

James David Bell, President
Incredible Speakers Bureau
Ph: (407) 297-1090
E-Mail: dave_bell@netwide.net

DEDICATION
• • • • • • •

To my family, friends and business colleagues,
whose names are too numerous to count,
who have all inspired me to write this book.

CONTENTS
• • • • • • •

Foreword 9
Introduction – What Prompted Me To Write This Book 11

PART I: TRUTHS

Guess What? If Your Life Is Out Of Whack
You Are Not Alone. 15
So How Does One Define Life Balance? 18
The Secret To Creating A More Balanced Lifestyle 21
Interview With Therese Kienast On How To Create
A More Meaningful And Fulfilling Life. 23
You Mean I Must Come To Grips With My Life Truths? 26
Interview With Mershon Shrigley On Balancing Roles
As Working Professional And Parent. 32
Interview With Christina Samaycia On Health And
Peak Performance. 36
Interview With Don Overbey On Effective Money
Management Habits. 40

PART II: CHOICES

Choices! 45
Life Direction Choice 48

PART III: ACTION

Chaos Management 61
Interview With Joy Loverde On How To Balance The Needs
Of Older Adult Parents With Our Other Time Demands 65
Attitude Management 75
Afterword – To Do's: A Baker's Dozen 81

Catch Your Balance And Run!

Foreword

● ● ● ● ● ● ●

This book is about maintaining a balanced lifestyle in the midst of these fast paced, and often paradoxical, times.

Catch Your Balance and Run! might sound like a contradiction in terms, but I think not. I am repeatedly struck by the speed at which our modern-day society moves. I am also struck by how unresourceful most people are when it comes to the balancing act; an act which when handled effectively ensures a sense of happiness in their lives.

In preparing this book, I have looked back over my years as a healthcare executive, spouse, parent, step-parent, entrepreneur and writer. I've had lengthy conversations with folks from all walks of life, and conducted numerous focus groups in an attempt to make sense of this topic for my participants as well as for myself. But mostly I have let my heart lead my mind where it will. I have wondered:

- why paying bills is so disruptive to my weekly routine
- why keeping a clean house is such a challenge to our family
- why success often leads to workaholism and often a lack of commitment to our other more important priorities in life
- why spirituality seems to be the answer to so many of our struggles and why so many of us are resistant to truly taking that complete "leap of faith."
- why any employee would tolerate a company that has little or no respect for their values and beliefs as well as their desire to live a meaningful and worthwhile life

…and so on.

All in all, you will find tons of ideas, and practical exercises within the pages of this book. The major foundational themes are TRUTHS, CHOICES, ACTION.

In other words, balance involves confronting those **TRUTHS** about who we are, what type of values we have and our purpose in life. This process enables us to make lifestyle **CHOICES** that are designed to ensure positive **ACTIONS** in our daily endeavors.

Being unbalanced, bedraggled, burned out and unfulfilled have never had much appeal to me. As I see it, keeping pace in the continual rat race of life will require us to paddle like never before; will require – again – the ability to *Catch Your Balance and Run!* It is my hope that the practical ideas from these pages will help you to reassess what is creating discord in your life, and assist you in moving toward bold and disciplined action.

I really had a ball putting this book together. Now I hope you have a ball reading it. By the way, one of the reasons I wrote this book is that I believe life is meant to be good! Outrageously a blast! A hoot! A journey comprised or encounters with truth and mystery, lifetime learning and constant surprise. But, to be brutally honest, I think such rewards will only be yours if you practice the lifestyle management strategy I call...

CATCH YOUR BALANCE AND RUN!

INTRODUCTION
• • • • • • •

What Prompted Me To Write This Book?

In order to tell you why I wrote this book, I need to take you back to the year 1986. I had just graduated from college in March and about a month later was hired for my first "real" job in the Human Resources Department at The Ohio State University Hospitals. Because my father had modeled hard work, dedication at all costs, and no handouts, I immediately fell into the trap I now affectionately refer to as *chronic professionalism*.

Since 64-hour work weeks were quickly the norm, I figured my career was on the fast track and it was now time to find a mate. With virtually no effort at all, a potential mate appeared out of the blue. So, on the day after Christmas 1987, I got married. This wedding, however, was a bit out of the ordinary in that it was a double wedding ceremony with my new bride and her twin sister and her new husband. This carefully orchestrated event was held in front of what seemed to be ten thousand people (although it was probably in the hundreds) with what seemed like an endless number of groomsmen, ministers, and nervous parents.

Within a few months of the wedding with my career now moving at warp speed, I received a call one day at work from an executive recruiter saying that he wanted to interview me for a Director of Human Resources position for an 89-bed hospital. After several conversations by phone with the recruiter, I determined that this position was worth an interview. I did have one lingering question in my mind, however, before exploring this opportunity further. Where is this job located? My head hit the desk in my office when the recruiter told me it was in Shelbyville, Indiana!

As a young black male, going into a small town in Indiana with a "ville" on the end of it conjured up memories of crosses being burned in yards and being run off the road by Klansmen clothed in white sheets. Nevertheless, I did interview and was selected for the position. I was pleasantly surprised to discover that the stereotypes that I had of Shelbyville were simply not true.

This new position provided me with the ambitious task of restoring a human resources department that had fallen woefully behind the times. My desire however, was to achieve great things for the department and impress the people who had made such a high investment to bring me over from Columbus, Ohio. This desire, however, led me to the point where I could not see straight from all the hours I was putting in.

Little did I know that this unhealthy work commitment was also the result of my unwillingness to deal with two painful issues which unexpectedly cropped up in the same year – namely the news that my Mother had been diagnosed with a very rare form of cancer, and the premature birth of my daughter, Amber.

Needless to say, the enormous stress associated with the premature birth, medical bills pouring in to the tune of $100,000, credit card charges I had racked up totaling over $20,000, two car payments totaling nearly $800 per month, the declining health and eventual death of my Mother, the breakup of my marriage, and the expectations I placed upon myself at work taught me some lessons about what is really important in life.

My reason for writing this book is to provide you with a ray of hope as you sort your way through the complexities of life. Even in what have appeared to be the worst possible circumstances in my life, I have been, and continue to be, hopeful. I may appear to be struggling on the outside, but I am winning on the inside. Why? Because I am always looking for ways to create more balance, meaning, and satisfaction in my life.

This does not mean that I don't have days when life isn't out of control. What it does mean is I refuse to be defeated by the rat race. So, if you are struggling with your juggling act today, or if you have a loved one who is, congratulations! This book is for YOU!

Part I
TRUTHS

Catch Your Balance And Run!

Guess What?
If Your Life Is Out Of Whack
You Are Not Alone

Many Americans are struggling not only with the accelerated pace of life, but with many of the social, demographic, and technological shifts that were predicted years ago by Alvin Toffler in his landmark book *Future Shock*. Recent studies indicate the following:

- According to the New York-based Work and Family Institute, approximately 7% of working Americans (1 in 4) say they care for an elderly relative, friend, or spouse. This same study indicates that within the next five years, 18% of us will be taking on the responsibility of caring for an older adult. It has been estimated more recently that 28% of employed family members quit their job prior to retirement to care for an aging relative.

- A Harris Survey indicated that the amount of leisure time enjoyed by the average American has decreased 37% since 1973. Over the same period, the average workweek, including commuting, has jumped from 40 hours to nearly 47 hours.

- In a recent Merrill Lynch study, 49% of their survey respondents acknowledged having more consumer debt (excluding mortgage payments) than savings; less than half of the respondents (41%) said they had a written household budget; while 40% said they did not have an emergency fund on hand in the event of a crises.

- A recent *Wall Street Journal* article entitled, "New York Hunters Ask Recruiters 'Is There Life After Work,'" indicated that questions about work-life balance are on the rise in job candidates' first-round talks with employers.

- A Yankelovich Monitor Survey found that 42% of working parents say they are spending less time with their spouses. One-third said they see more tension in their marriages.

- The American Society of Chartered Life Underwriters and Chartered Financial Consultants found that balancing work and family life was the top source of workplace pressure for about 75% of men and women.

- Many high profile executives, from Pepsi-Cola North America's CEO Brenda Barnes to former Department of Labor Secretary Robert Reich, have walked away from prestigious jobs to be with their families.

> *You see and understand what is right but refuse to act on it. You hear but don't really listen.*
> – Isaiah 42:19-20

So what are some of the possible consequences of ignoring your call to a more balanced life?

Health Problems: The American Academy of Family Physicians estimates that two-thirds of all visits to family physicians are the result of stress related symptoms. Experts tell us that poor dietary habits, lack of exercise, and insufficient rest are taking a toll on us.

Frequent Relationship Conflicts: Our busy lives leave us with minimal time to nurture relationships with family, friends and other important people in our lives. Studies, in fact, tell us that the average American couple spends less than five minutes a day in meaningful conversation.

Life Becomes Meaningless: While many of us are seeking more meaningful lives, in reality we are drifting further and further away from this goal as our busy lives leave us with so little time to reflect on what is truly important.

Irrational Decisions: The great evangelist Charles Swindoll once remarked, "Wise decisions seldom can occur in a hurry." There is no doubt that the pace of life has led to some life choices that we later regreted.

Children Modeling Your Lifestyle: Kids are very much a product of the environment in which they have been raised. Thus, if they only see you working long hours while neglecting other more important priorities, they are likely to model these same behaviors later in life.

Distracted Mind: We can all relate to how unproductive our lives become when we are focused on too many things. Moreover, as situations like driving to work without remembering how we got to our destination, become more common, we truly put our very lives in jeopardy.

So How Does One Define Life Balance?

Whenever someone asks me this question, the first thought that runs through my mind is that they are seeking clues as to how I define balance in my own life? Sarcastically they will often challenge me further by asking, "So what's a balanced life really look like to you?" "How is it supposed to feel?" "Is a sixty-hour work week a true indicator of an unbalanced lifestyle?" "Isn't balance an impossibility in a world which demands so much of us?"

Let me attempt to address these most important questions by first sharing with you a few comments from an informal survey we conducted asking people "how they defined life balance." The responses were rather fascinating:

- Being well rounded in all areas of your life – spiritual, physical and mental
- The search for moderation
- Making all of your roles "fit" without having any one of them consume you or throw you out of balance
- Freedom from anxiety
- Balancing work, friends, church, God as well as doing things for self
- Happiness
- Time for everything I love to do
- Satisfaction with all aspects of my life

Then we did a bit more digging with our survey questions by asking the respondents, "If you could change one thing to create more balance in your life, what would it be?" We received the following responses:

- More time
- Retire
- Job
- Less Work
- More time for family
- Assume control over my work schedule
- Add more hours to the day. . .Ha!
- At 5:30 PM every weekday, the power would go out at the office, thus forcing me to get on with my personal life
- Cut out required reading
- Strong commitment to Christ
- My house would stay clean
- Be more organized

OK! Enough with what everyone else says! You are probably chopping at the bit wondering what my definition of balance is. Well, here it is:

> Balance is a state of meaningful existence which occurs when we bring into alignment **our personal truths, life choices, and actions.**

So Why Is This State So Difficult To Achieve?

Because if you are like me, you struggle with whether life should primarily involve being proactive or reactive. In fact, you can probably relate to the struggle identified in the chart on the next page.

Unfortunately, most of us place our greatest emphasis on doing, on an "activity equals results" mentality. Our whole self-esteem often becomes contingent on our work, existing in a continual state of busyness. We therefore become a *"human doing"* rather than a *"human being."*

THE TUG AND PULL OF LIFE

PROACTIVE	or	**REACTIVE**
Doing	or	Being
Action	or	Meditation
Serious	or	Fun
Being God	or	Seeking God
Speaking	or	Listening
Fast	or	Slow
Joy	or	Sorrow
Applying	or	Learning
Productivity	or	Recreation

The Secret To Creating A More Balanced Lifestyle

Creating a more balanced lifestyle begins with an honest assessment of yourself based on the two questions listed below. Take a moment right now and find a quiet place to reflect and respond to these questions in the space provided.

QUESTION NUMBER 1: My definition of life balance is:

_____

_____

_____

_____

QUESTION NUMBER 2: My biggest life balance challenges are (describe them in as much detail as possible):

_____

_____

_____

_____

Now, did you answer the questions or were you too lazy to jot down your thoughts? If you did not answer the questions, I urge you to go back and complete the exercise. If you did, great! Let's take a moment now to explore the meaning behind these two questions.

Question 1, which asks for your personal definition of life balance, is an important question to reflect on in that it provides some insight into how various life-influences condition the choices you regularly make. For example, the way I view life balance has been largely influenced over the years by my Father, and the tremendous sense of meaning he found in his work. As a result, I tend to define my reality around my vocation as a speaker and writer. The problem comes when I loose touch of the effect of this choice on my life, as well as its impact on my family. I now know that if I fail to take time to tune into this reality regularly, things begin to reel out of control (i.e., neglecting to spend time with family, poor eating habits).

While assisting a corporate client with a work/family consulting project recently, I had the opportunity to chat with the President regarding the 70-hour work weeks that he consistently puts in. He commented that he did not view this as excessive because of the enjoyment he derived from his work. Then, in revealing his guilty conscience, he went on to mention that he schedules at least one round of golf each week, a leisure activity, he says, helps to relieve the stress associated with this role and responsibility. When I asked him about how he carves out time for his wife and kids, his response was, "My wife and I have an unusual agreement regarding my work commitments. Although we spend little time together, she has accepted my role as primary breadwinner for the family. This arrangement has worked extremely well for us over the past 17 years."

While, in a sense, I could relate to the love he had for his work, my mind kept reflecting back on whether his chronic workaholism was having a negative effect on his marriage. Ironically, the individual he preceded as President, is now chairman of the parent company and works a very limited schedule. He was forced to make major lifestyle modifications after suffering a heart attack a few years ago.

Do you get the message? The choices we make regarding how to define balance, typically have corresponding consequences, and that effectively handling this give-and-take is the key to keeping life in its proper perspective.

The second question, "What are my biggest life balance challenges," should bring to the surface those truths that need to be directly dealt with in order for you to create a more meaningful life. You probably know what these major challenges are, but you have chosen to either deny that they exist in hopes that they will disappear, or beat yourself up over your lack of success in handling them in the past. Here is the key to handling these challenges:

> *You must maintain a state of awareness of those areas that are creating disharmony in your life and simply **act on what you know** with your heart rather than your head.*

If you find yourself stuck as to how to move forward with the changes you need to make, I encourage you to consider engaging the ongoing assistance of an accountability partner or professional coach. These individuals can give you great encouragement in pursuing your goals, and are adept in telling you what you need to hear – not necessarily what you want to hear. Check out the following interview for more details.

• • • • • • •

Interview With Therese Kienast On How To Create A More Meaningful And Fulfilling Life

Therese is the founder of People Builders, Schaumburg, IL, a firm that provides one-on-one personal/professional coaching services to individuals who want to reprogram their life for success.

Michael: Therese, why does it appear that so many people have lost sight of who they really are?

Therese: Often it is the result of their denial of the painful realities in their life. Consequently they end up living in a lost, confused, unfocused manner.

Michael: So what steps should they consider in their efforts to create a more balanced, meaningful existence?

Therese: Obviously, the route to a more balanced lifestyle is going to vary somewhat from person to person. In general though, those that have achieved this lifestyle have acknowledged at some point their self-limiting beliefs and use them as a basis for meaningful change.

For example, if you tell me that your job is making you ill on a regular basis, I might ask you to tell me what it looks like or feels like to go into work each day. Through this process of inquiry, the hope is that you will acknowledge the pain associated with what you are feeling and begin to take steps toward putting yourself in a healthier situation.

Michael: In other words, you are saying that the knowledge to implement change and create more meaning and balance in life is already inside each of us? That we already know the route to take but we need to acknowledge it? Am I understanding you correctly?

Therese: That's right. Healthy change becomes a matter of acting on what you already know.

Michael: Taking action seems like the difficult part – painful too at times.

Therese: Right, again! In his best selling book, *The Road Less Traveled*, M. Scott Peck reminds us of a very important truth, "life is difficult." He goes on to say that it is only through acceptance of this reality that we are able to move forward with meaningful change in our life.

Michael: What else holds us back from making the difficult changes we know we need to make?

Therese: I believe our difficulties often arise when we make decisions from the head and not the heart. In fact, I have a term for those voices in our mind that lead us astray. I call them "gremlins." I help my coaching clients to recognize their gremlins so they won't control their lives.

I believe that every person's strength comes from tapping into their heart and spirit – that all-knowing part of ourselves. Those of us who listen to our hearts discover an aliveness, an energy, and connectedness that transcends any ups and downs that we may face. We begin to affirm those talents, skills, abilities and gifts that allow us to be all that God calls us to be.

Michael: So your role as a coach is to help us show up and be who we really are?

Therese: Exactly! In fact, I tell my clients, "You hired me to follow your agenda." My greatest hope for you is that you will grant yourself permission to just show up just as you are. Trusting that you already have the answers, it is just a matter of owning them. My goal is to help you let go of your yesterdays and embrace your Godly gifts today.

● ● ● ● ● ● ●

You Mean I Must Come To Grips With What's Really Important In My Life?

Yes, you must come to grips with your inner truths. As the Bible verse says, "the truth will set you free!" Let's examine this thought a bit more.

Below are seven foundational values that play a significant role in your life. Please take a moment to indicate which three are of the highest value to you currently – the three that you are currently investing most of your time, energy and attention to right now. Remember, you are indicating which three are priorities for you right now, not what you would ideally like them to be.

```
( ) Your Romantic Life
( ) Your Spiritual Life
( ) Your Personal Growth
( ) Your Job
( ) Your Family Life
( ) Your Health and Wellness
( ) Your Financial Situation
```

Now that you have completed this exercise, let's explore why prioritizing each of these areas of your life is important.

1. ROMANTIC LIFE/MEANINGFUL RELATIONSHIPS

You would probably agree that meaningful, loving relationships with others are important. Why is it then that we often find ourselves in unhealthy relationships that contribute stress and imbalance in our lives? Why does the average American couple spend less than four minutes a day in meaningful conversation when virtually every expert on relationships is telling us how important communication is?

One day in the midst of one of those valleys that all married people go through, it occurred to me how little time I was taking to nurture the relationship with my wife, Angie. I stopped what I was doing at the moment, opened my calendar organizer and began to look at my daily schedules over the past six months. Lo and behold, I found that while all of my various work commitments had been meticulously scheduled on those deluxe Franklin Planner® pages, there was not the least bit of mention given to scheduling time with my wife.

Since discovering this painful truth, I have committed myself to taking more time out of my busy schedule to spend with Angie – whether it be lunch or dinner together once a week, or a week-long vacation in Tahoe.

While this noble goal has recently become more challenging (at the time of this writing, Angie is enrolled in law school at Notre Dame – a journey that is consuming a great deal of her time) we now realize more than ever how critically important it is for us to set aside time to be together.

A QUICK GUT CHECK!

What do you need to do in order to nurture meaningful relationships in your life? If you are frequently away from home due to work, you may want to consider a 45-minute phone call to your spouse every evening or schedule a regular date night when you are home.

Think of a fun activity that the two of you can share from time-to-time; like hopping in the car one weekend and driving to a city you know nothing about and spending time there, or going to a fancy restaurant. Or you might want to buy that special person a card with a message from you, just because.

2. SPIRITUAL LIFE

Undoubtedly one of the reasons that spiritualism is sweeping this nation at an unprecedented rate is that many of us are recognizing that we need to trust in One greater than ourselves to assist us with this endless juggling act. One of my favorite Bible stories relating to work/life balance is found in Luke 10:38-42. It reads:

> As Jesus and the disciples continued on their way to Jerusalem, they came to a village where a woman named Martha welcomed them into her home. Her sister, Mary, sat at the Lord's feet, listening to what he taught. But Martha was worrying over the big dinner she was preparing. She came to Jesus and said, "Lord, doesn't it seem unfair to you that my sister just sits here while I do all the work? Tell her to come and help me."
>
> But the Lord said to her, "My dear Martha, you are so upset over all these details! There is really only one thing worth being concerned about. Mary has discovered it, and I won't take it away from her."

Isn't that a great story? If you are like me, you probably try to emulate Martha from time-to-time forgetting what the Lord is trying to get across to you here, that we need to just be there for Him and He will take care of the details!

One of the most important activities that I am learning to embrace on a consistent basis is consistent prayer. In those moments where I am trying to be all things to all people, I ask the Lord to help me sort out what is important from that which is trivial. Unfortunately, what we often do is to pursue what we think is best without consulting the Lord. Then we find ourselves running to Him for advice on how to release the pressure, or change the scenario.

A QUICK GUT CHECK!

Think about where you are spiritually. Ask yourself, "Am I taking the time to fellowship with other spiritually-minded people and commune with God on a regular basis? Am I so busy that when God is shouting at me with the wisdom I need to live a more balanced life, that it falls on deaf ears? One of the best spiritual resources on the market to assist you in reclaiming a sense of balance in today's turbocharged world (in addition to the Bible) is a book entitled *Margin: Restoring Emotional, Physical, Financial, and Time Reserves to Overloaded Lives*, by Richard A. Swenson, MD (ISBN 0-89109-888-7).

3. PERSONAL GROWTH

Several years ago during my initial few months as a struggling entrepreneur, I had the privilege of hearing Jim Rohn, who many consider to be one of the top five personal growth speakers in the world. I remember that day well. I had a perplexing question on my mind on which I hoped Jim could provide some perspective. That question was "how does an ambitious entrepreneur, like me, balance those long work hours that are necessary for any start-up business with those other important life priorities – like family, leisure time, church activities, etc.

About halfway through his speech, Jim said something that not only motivated me to consider cutting back on the enormous number of hours I was working, but allowed me to simultaneously enhance my profits as a company. He remarked, that, "True success occurs when you work harder on yourself than you do on your job. If you work hard on your job you will make a living. But, if you work hard on yourself, you can make a fortune!" My interpretation of what he said is:

> *Personal growth allows you to become more valuable to the marketplace thereby allowing you to make more money in a vocation where you can work fewer hours!*

A QUICK GUT CHECK!

Think about the last 12 months. Are you working more hours and discovering less and less time for other pursuits? How might you enhance your value to the world by investing in the necessary personal growth books, audio learning systems, and courses? Would committing to more renewal activities such as vacations, and regular exercise make a difference in your overall happiness, productivity and ultimate well-being?

4. YOUR JOB

It is no secret that we spend most of our working hours at our jobs. Unfortunately, most Americans when asked will tell you that they are moderately to very unhappy with the job they are in. In fact, one recent survey found that one in six workers thought about quitting daily. And when you tie that in with work/life issues, 42% of Americans surveyed in a Baxter Healthcare study indicated that they were looking for another job because of a work/life conflict!

The message? It is not only important for you to find meaning in your work, but to identify the type of work environment that upholds the work/family values that you hold. Clearly, if you are unhappy and unfulfilled in your work life, these same feelings are likely to spill over into your personal life as well.

An interesting article in the *Wall Street Journal* suggests that job seekers are increasingly taking another look at companies that fail to respect their needs and wants outside of work. The article's author, discussed a surprising trend on undergraduate campuses. Questions about work/life balance are surfacing in job candidates first round talks with employers. What this tells me is that in today's booming economy and tight labor market, it may pay to explore your options and pursue the type of workplace environment that encourages a healthy balance between your work and life priorities.

A QUICK GUT CHECK!

Do you work in an environment which not only allows for meaningful work but also provides you the flexibility to enjoy family, church, leisure activities and the other priorities in your life? Go to the library or use the Internet to look up information on "family friendly" companies. Take time to talk with a trusted friend, mentor, personal coach, or career counselor about your options. More importantly, make changes if your job is preventing you from living the life you want.

5. FAMILY

We all want quality time with family and loved ones. If you are like me, however, you may be feeling a bit guilty about the amount of attention your professional career is getting verses time with your family. Your job gets the majority of your attention on any one given day. While such thoughts are uncomfortable, it is important that we reflect on how essential we are to our families and vice versa.

At the very moment that I am writing this section of the book my mind is pondering the travel schedule I will embark upon over the next several weeks. My itinerary reads: From South Bend, Indiana, to Springfield, Illinois, to Green Bay, Wisconsin, to Cincinnati, Ohio, to Phoenix, Arizona, to Minneapolis, Minnesota, to an entire week in Florida, and then back to Minneapolis.

I begin to wonder how will this time away impact my relationship with my family? Should I quit work and pray for money, or should I hang in there knowing that ultimately it will be for the greater good of the family?

One summer a few years ago, there were well over 200 heat-related deaths reported in Chicago. This tragedy was due to the high temperatures, as well as the lack of air conditioning in many of the older dwellings. Every night the television news made pleas to Chicago residents to check in on loved ones, particularly those who were elderly and homebound, to ensure that they were in a cool environment. Unfortunately, it seemed like the death toll continued to mount each day until the heat finally abated. When the final count was made and the demographic profiles of the victims were compiled, there was one startling discovery. In a city with one of the largest Hispanic populations in the United States, there was not one heat-related death within the Hispanic community. Social Scientists believe that his unusual occurrence was the result of the fact that family life is viewed higher than any other value in the Hispanic culture.

A QUICK GUT CHECK!

Recall the last time you felt a bit guilty about your lack of commitment to your family. Were you open with your family members regarding your struggles in balancing work and family? Are there any close friends you can turn to with regards to gaining some fruitful advice on keeping this work/family struggle in its proper perspective?

● ● ● ● ● ● ●

Interview With Mershon Shrigley On Balancing Roles As Working Professional And Parent

Mershon Shrigley is President of Shrigley & Associates, Schaumburg, IL, a marketing/communications organization specializing in newsletters.

Michael: Mershon, as a parent and small business owner, what are some keys you have discovered that help you juggle multiple responsibilities while keeping your life in its proper perspective?

Mershon: One of the most useful steps I took a few years ago was to write a personal mission statement. To do this, I followed the lead of Covey in his book *Seven Habits of Highly Effective People*. This statement helps me keep what's important in my life in perspective – my relationship with God, my family, health, and helping others. As a small business owner, keeping what's important in view (physically written down) keeps me focused.

Michael: So, in other words, this defining statement keeps you on track.

Mershon: Exactly. As a home-based business, it is very important for me to maintain strong boundaries with my clients. Keeping my life in perspective helps me work an eight-to-five day and keep my weekends free for my family and other interests.

Michael: What thought can you share with the single mom who is at her wits end trying to juggle endless responsibilities?

Mershon: My advise is simple – take charge of your life. Don't let others bombard you with their priorities; this includes your children. Set limits with friends, relatives, clients and even yourself. There are many wonderful opportunities in the world, the important thing is to choose carefully what you love to do and what you can do well, given the time you have. Don't try to be all things to all people.

Michael: You have raised three great kids – most of the time as a single mom. What is the key?

Mershon: As in all relationships, I believe the key comes down to quality communications; which take time. When I started my business 13 years ago, my children were ages 14, 9 and 3. After school, each one in turn would come into my home office and tell me about their day. I took the time, right then, to listen. They would soon be off doing their own thing and I would be back to work. This was the basis for their positive self-esteem; showing them that what was happening in their life and how they were feeling was important to me – and still is!

I believe that creating structure and consistency is also very important. We always have breakfast and dinner together at the table with no television, telephone, or other interruptions. This ritual has been a foundation for our family communications. We stay in touch with each other's daily lives. Having a quick pizza in front of the television just isn't a basis for staying in touch and communicating what's important.

Michael: What else can you share concerning how you keep your life in order?

Mershon: Keeping fiscally fit is another priority for me. I have always followed the philosophy of not spending more than I make. In fact, I believe the key is spending less than you earn while saving and giving away a significant percentage. Securing my future is very important to me. Many years ago I found an excellent financial planner who has helped me set up investment programs that will safeguard my future. Giving money as well as time to my church and community are also very important to me. I have been a volunteer since I was 12-years-old and I have learned that when you throw your bread out on the waters of life, it comes back buttered.

I have worked on helping my children be fiscally fit also by giving them allowances from the time they were very young. They started buying their own clothes when they were twelve. They know how much they have each month to spend and they must learn to budget accordingly.

No matter what your financial status (rich or poor or in-between), I believe that having your finances in order frees you up to do the more exciting, creative things with your family.

∙ ∙ ∙ ∙ ∙ ∙ ∙

6. HEALTH AND WELLNESS

Mark Victor Hanson, co-author of the mega best-selling book series Chicken Soup for the Soul, firmly believes that one of the keys to a meaningful and exuberant life is the care we give to our bodies. The human body is amazing in that it has the ability to protect, adapt, function and repair itself simultaneously. However, in order for this to occur on a consistent basis, there must be a proper ratio of nourishment, exercise, and rest, all combined with a positive mental attitude.

Keeping your "insides" in balance provides you with more energy for your daily endeavors. In particular, we need to pay more attention to our gut.

Barb Schwarz, author of the powerful book entitled, *If You Wear Out Your Body, Where Will You Live?*, challenges us to get our bodies back in their proper balance by examining the number of BOWEL MOVEMENTS WE ARE HAVING EACH DAY! "Proper bowel function entails having two to three good bowel movements each day," says Barb. Most people who are not aware of this go through their lives eliminating once a day, once every other day, or less. Often this results when we fail to get enough water and fiber in our diet. . .two necessities to rid our bodies of toxins. Barb asks, "If you eat three meals a day and only eliminate once a day, where are the other two meals hiding?"

So how does this all relate to work/life balance? It is my belief that one of the reasons many of us lead an unbalanced life is because we lack the energy to pursue the values that are important to us. This lack of energy is often the result of a lifestyle and dietary habit that perpetuates faulty digestion and elimination. When we do not eliminate our waste properly, toxins back up in our system which causes self-poisoning; a condition which lowers our overall feelings of health and vitality. P.S. – Sorry to be so descriptively blunt but this is something many of us overlook!

A QUICK GUT CHECK!

Given your overall levels of health, would it be useful for you to design a fun, easy to implement plan for exercise and diet? Have you incorporated some simple routine into your day, such as using the stairs versus elevators, drinking 8-12 glasses of water each day, and taking a multi-vitamin formula? Take a close look at what you can reasonably accomplish each day in the midst of your busy workday. You might want to invest in a fitness coach or partner with someone who will help keep you accountable to the health commitments you make.

• • • • • • •

Interview With Christina Samaycia On Health And Peak Performance

Christina Samaycia is President of Wellness Innovations, a firm specializing in corporate wellness programs.

Michael: Christina, one of the biggest frustrations that many of us face is carving out enough time to exercise and eat properly. What suggestions do you have for those of us who struggle with this important priority?

Christina: In order to make these healthy lifestyle choices, we must first of all acknowledge how important they are to our well-being. We know that proper exercise and nutrition can have a dramatic impact on a variety of health issues including cardiovascular disease, cancer, and our daily energy. Unfortunately, however, many of us wait for those "moments of truth" – such as heart attacks or cancer – before making substantive lifestyle changes.

Michael: So, are there some basic rules of thumb that we can follow once we've committed ourselves to making diet and exercise a priority?

Christina: Sure. Number one – <u>keep it simple</u>! For example, studies tell us that a minimum of 20 to 30 minutes of exercise a day is satisfactory. You can accomplish this by walking a half-hour at lunch, riding your exercise bike while watching the evening news, or while at work taking the stairs several times a day, rather than the elevator. I often suggest to my clients that they schedule exercise on their calendars just like they would schedule a business meeting or even an appointment with their hairstylist.

Second, if at all possible, schedule your exercise time in the morning. If you leave it to the end of the day the tendency will be to replace this activity with something else.

Third, have fun! Pick an exercise routine or activity you enjoy. Find a friend to workout with you so you can keep each other accountable.

Michael: By 2 PM my energy level usually begins to wane. I find that I don't have that extra burst of energy necessary to take care of those remaining priorities on my daily list. Any ideas?

Christina: Mike, achieving peak energy levels is directly tied to four things. One, appropriate exercise! The best exercise is rhythmic in nature such as walking or running.

Second, eat healthy foods. Ideally, carbohydrates should represent 55-60% of your total daily intake, protein at 15%, and fat 25% or less. This involves a diet comprised of whole grains, fruits, vegetables, fish and poultry. If at all possible, avoid saturated fats.

Third, drink 8-12 glasses of water a day to rid your body of the toxins that can cause numerous health problems. By the way, water doesn't include coffee, tea, or soda. Bottled and purified water are the best.

Fourth, your energy levels will increase when you effectively manage your stress. Effective stress management steps include regular exercise, breathing properly, and meditation. If you've got a little extra money each month, you might even want to treat yourself to a regular massage from a massage therapist.

Michael: You've had a personal success story with regards to weight management. Tell us a little about what you've learned from this experience.

Christina: Experience has taught me that losing weight is the easy part. Keeping it off is what's difficult. My advice to anyone who is trying to loose and/or maintain their ideal weight is to be persistent. Despite what the so-called experts tell us, the only real secret to weight loss is proper nutrition and regular exercise.

Michael: Let's conclude by exploring the whole issue of a proper diet. What advice do you have for those of us who are constantly on the run and don't eat well?

Christina: Don't make it so difficult for yourself. Cook enough healthy food on the weekend to have leftovers to eat during the week. Keep healthy snacks on hand. Carry a bottle of purified water with you while you're on the run. Make smart decisions on what you put in your body. It will make a "huge" difference in how you feel mentally and physically.

● ● ● ● ● ● ●

7. FINANCIAL SITUATION

If you have been asking yourself, "How can I maintain a reasonable lifestyle today when my financial well-being is in a constant state of distress?" then you are not alone. In a recent study conducted by Merrill Lynch, nearly 49% of the respondents said that their consumer debt (not including mortgage payments or home equity loans) exceeds their savings. On average, the survey respondents said they allocated 21% of their income toward paying non-mortgage consumer debt.

Clearly, life becomes more fulfilling when your daily thoughts and decisions are not centered on "how am I going to pay the bills or when will I get enough money to take a vacation?" Unfortunately, one of the main reasons many of us find ourselves in debt is because we overspend in the name of trying to fulfill some personal unmet need. This pattern often results in "too much month at the end of the money." I challenge you to take the necessary steps to get out of debt. Then begin to live within your means by making sound investments that will give you security in the future. Direct some of the money that was previously used for frills towards sound investments that will make life more secure over the long run.

A QUICK GUT CHECK!

In the next month, make plans to review your financial objectives with a financial advisor. Determine whether the debt you are carrying is appropriate or if it would be wise to scale back on your expenses through a consolidation loan, etc. If you have not taken a vacation in a while or been able to enjoy some of your favorite leisure activities due to a tight financial situation, set a goal today for how much you are going to save each month in order to enjoy life more fully. Also, be sure to explore savings and investment options as a way of securing your future.

Interview With Don Overbey On How We Can Develop Effective Money Management Habits

Don is a financial advisor with American Express Financial Advisors, Wilmette, Illinois.

Michael: Don, why is it that so many of us have what could be referred to as "more month left at the end of the money," rather than visa versa?

Don: First of all, we mistakenly believe that managing money is a piece of cake once we've earned it. Unfortunately, many of the habits we develop concerning money are a product of our upbringing, We unwittingly follow in our parents' footsteps.

Michael: So, you believe that the environment in which we were raised often contributes to our poor money management habits.

Don: Yes. And once we're entrenched in these unhealthy behaviors such as carrying large balances on our credit cards, it is difficult to change the pattern. As a colleague of mine aptly put it, "You can't talk yourself out of what you behaved yourself into."

Michael: So Don, what are some of the money management habits we need to develop to prevent our finances from getting out of control?

Don: Perhaps the most important thing we can do for ourselves is to "salt away" a portion of each pay check. Ten percent is the generally accepted rule of thumb to use when determining how much to set aside. We should also get into the habit of using cash for our purchases whenever possible.

Michael: Any advise for planning for the long term?

Don: Undoubtedly, the best rule to follow is to begin with your future goals in mind and work backwards. For example, if you are 33-years-old and want to retire at 40 with $750,000 in the bank, you will need to determine how much you need to set aside each month to accomplish this goal, then begin to plan your savings and investments accordingly.

• • • • • • •

Part II
CHOICES

Catch Your Balance And Run!

Choices!

> *"Act On What You Already Know"* – Michael Scott

Your heart already knows what to do. That's right! You've been receiving powerful messages from your heart saying, "_____(**your name**), you know it is time to make some lifestyle changes. So maybe it's time to quit trying to just get by. Act on what you know!" You will discover a life that is more meaningful, worthwhile and balanced.

Why is it that instead of listening to those powerful messages from your heart, you follow your head – a habit that often causes you to devise cleaver excuses to justify an unbalanced lifestyle. By the way, I'm not trying to be self righteous here as I reflect back on my own experiences with *excusitis*, these come to mind:

- Gee, I hate balancing this stupid checkbook! I'll just continue to write checks and guess what's in the account. Besides, if I overdraw the account, my overdraft protection will kick in.

- A one-week vacation? Come on! My work schedule is way too busy. Besides, as a small business owner, who's going to handle things while I'm away?

- One cup of coffee and a sweet roll will get me through the day. It's impossible to eat well while I'm on the run. I just don't have time to fit in exercise and besides, I am 5 foot 11 inches 160 pounds, so I must be healthy.

- Sit and watch a movie with my wife? You have gotta be kidding! My job is to provide income for this household. I need to get working tonight and not goof off.

- Four hours of sleep is enough for me. Hey, J. Paul Getty said that the key to business success is to get "up early, stay up late, strike oil!"

- I'll spend time with God in prayer if and when things take a turn for the worse. I just don't know how all of these "spiritual people" find time to read their Bible in the morning and pray throughout the day.

- I must get these 50 items that are on my calendar done today! I know I have listed them all as "A" priorities, but I should be able to whiz through them all with no problem.

Does this dialogue sound familiar? Has it occurred to you that many of the lifestyle habits you dislike about others are a part of your life? Isn't it time to admit to yourself that enough is enough – that the quality of your life involves making choices that are in alignment with your true self?

I INVITE YOU TO WALK WITH ME ON A SPIRITUAL JOURNEY

I truly believe in the philosophy that "life is a journey – not the final destination." The remaining pages of this book are devoted to your making some meaningful choices in the evolution of your life. My greatest joy will be to see you embrace those "choices of the heart" – choices that reflect a sense of integrity with yourself as well as for others. Your choices, by the way, must focus on those things that you ultimately have a measure of control over. In unlocking the keys to a life that "is meant to be good," it's important to keep in mind that you may not be able to change how your parents raised you, or personality traits of your children which causes them to rebel against your parenting, or a divorce that you didn't want which left you financially ruined, or parents who require your attention. You can, however, change yourself, your philosophy of life, and the way that you respond to the inevitable challenges that are part of your everyday existence.

M. Scott Peck in his best-selling book *The Road Less Traveled*, said it best when he remarked that, "Life is difficult." What he is telling us is that you will never be able to move forward with the task of effectively managing your life until you come to grips with this truth.

> *"Your inward attitude does not have to reflect your outward circumstances."* – Michael Scott

Life Direction Choice

Do you find yourself drawn to that rare person who seems to have his or her life in order and wonder why you can't get there too? Do you admire those individuals who have a plan for where their life is headed and wish you could tap into the wisdom that keeps them on a steady course? Have you ever read an article in your local paper or perused a book that caused you to reflect on where you are and where you want to head in your life endeavors? Do you wake up in the morning and say to yourself, "I need to do more to make each day count!"

If the answer to any one of these questions is "yes" then congratulations, you are ready to tap into your true self and discover how to expand, refine, and nurture your life direction.

There is an old saying that "energy without direction is just waste." I have always suspected that the major reason why so many people are steering through life asleep at the wheel is because they have no plan as to where they are headed. My point is not to offer a panacea for setting your life on course. Rather, it's to empower you to reflect on the impact that your life choices can have relative to positioning your future.

Just like the question "what is your final destination" that is posed to you when you check your bags with the Skycap at the airport, you need to reflect on the direction of your whole life. Ask yourself, as pilot of your life, whether you're cleared for a safe landing, or, in the words of Therese Kienast President of People Builders, "flying in a holding pattern." Unfortunately, as you examine how you're handling the chaos in your life, you may discover that you are running out of gas and are going to need to radio the control tower for an emergency landing.

The good news is that creating a sense of focus and balance in your life is truly possible. Wherever you are in your current life experience, you can design a life beyond what you have previously imagined or dreamed.

You *can* maintain a rewarding and satisfying career while creating a happy, healthy environment at home. You *can* enjoy magical vacations and leisure pursuits that renew your mind, soul and spirit in the midst of a busy professional life. You *can* channel your attention to nurturing meaningful relationships while keeping your other life priorities in check. If you hear that a balanced lifestyle is a lost cause, don't believe it. Be assured that you *can* revitalize your life and take it to new heights.

As we approach the year 2000, along with many other experts, I too believe that the path to a more directed, balanced life is a spiritual one. Instead of asserting ourselves as an island unto ourselves, the best way to create balance is to focus your attention on the life that you want and then release the struggle to God. As the old saying goes, "do not feel totally, personally, irrevocably, responsible for everything. That's my job. Love God."

Those of us who are able to keep life in its proper perspective quickly realize that the less we struggle with putting together the perfect response to our life questions, the more our path begins to unfold. What many of us are guilty of is trying to force life to conform to what we want it to be, versus allowing it to unfold within the Lord's Divine Order. Often this mindset creates an internal discord that leads us to try to control everything, to try to be all things to all people, and to seek the approval and avoid the disapproval of others – all in the name of an unmet need that has not been addressed.

Years ago, while I was in grade school, the seeds of my nature – a nature that led me to seek the approval of others in an unhealthy way – was revealed to me by my best friend, Michael Bennett. While we were in high school one day in the midst of one of our conversations, he blurted out, "Michael you are so selfless. You care about others more than you care about yourself. That's going to come back and haunt you one day." His words turned out to be right. As a result of ignoring the realities of my lifestyle, my world revolved around trying to be pleasing to others all the time.

> *"I don't know what the key to success is, but I'm convinced that the key to failure is trying to please everybody!"* – Bill Cosby

Now it's time for you to examine your calling. Use the questions below as a guide. By the way, your outcomes will be increased 100 fold if you solicit the help of a spouse, friend, success team, or professional coach. Often they will help you come to grips with not necessarily what you want to hear, but what you need to hear.

QUESTIONS UPON WHICH TO REFLECT AND TO ACT:

- Are you involved in a type of work that provides you with meaning and allows you to maintain a sense of integrity with yourself as it relates to your other life priorities? If no, describe the type of life you envision and the reasons why this lifestyle would be ideally suited to you.

- Write down what you believe to be your calling. Are you pursuing it, at least in some small way? Does your current work situation allow you to take advantage of your calling? If yes, please describe the way in which it does? What do you want your friends, relatives, co-workers, to say about you when your days are over? What type of lasting legacy do you want to leave for our friends and loved ones?

> *"The biggest pain in life is regret."* – Mickey's Mom

ARE THERE ANY KEYS TO ASSIST IN CREATING A SENSE OF LIFE DIRECTION?

This is one of the most common questions that surfaces in my workshops and seminars. To the person that asks the question, I frequently ask them whether they are willing to step into some realities about their life that may be a bit uncomfortable. As I often say, "the truth will set you free, but first if may make you miserable."

In these next few pages I would like to expose you to three fundamental traits that I have found common among those who have created a meaningful life – individuals who have been able to consistently catch their balance and keep relative pace with today's ever- changing world. By incorporating these building blocks into your daily routine, you will discover a wellspring from which to draw inspiration, creative ideas, and solutions to the many obstacles that are a part of finding your path.

LIFE DIRECTION KEY NO. 1 – NURTURE YOUR CALLING

The irony about life direction is that in large part it has already been scripted for us by God. We all have talents, skills, abilities and gifts that allow for passionate living and life focus if we will simply allow them to unfold. What we are all facing here is aptly summed up by Howard Thurman, a noted academic, when he stated, "The paradox that is at the heart of all experiences is the mysterious marriage of choice and surrender, individual freedom and the acceptance of ones destiny."

A purpose or calling, as I see it, is present when your loving desire to serve others brings you a sense of passion, a sense of joy, a sense of meaning in life. In other words, your life work is in alignment with those things in life that you value most. Once you have identified your calling you will often find that you will lead a more balanced life. This is because you have connected with your true self. Excitement will come through examing the "whys" in your life (i.e., why do I work 60 hours per week; why am I experiencing the hardships of life) realizing if you have a why for life, you can accomplish almost any "how!"

LIFE DIRECTION KEY NO. 2 – HONOR YOUR VALUES

Values help define who you are. They are those characteristics that are most important to you. Broken down into priorities, they can guide your daily activities. They are the lifeblood of a truly balanced life.

For a number of years now, I have struggled with determining what is most important in my life. I find that my values continue to evolve as I get older, wiser and more hurried in my life activities. Along the way, I have learned a few lessons that I believe have widespread applicability.

1. Quit trying to make everything important – The key word is "everything." Only a few individuals I have come in contact with seem to be directing their energy towards a short list of values that they deem as being truly important. The rest of us find ourselves locked in a day-to-day game called "value conflict" which causes our lives to veer out of control. We have what is affectionately known as "monkey mind," that common malady that causes us to jump from one thing to the next like a monkey leaps in the air from tree to tree. The reality is that we are better off focusing on those values which allow us to truly make a difference – not only in our lives, but in the lives of others.

2. Recognize that it's OK for your values to change over time – Defining your values is a process that is in a constant state of evolution. Accept your values for what they currently are realizing that they are likely to change as you continue along on your life's journey.

3. Use your values to set goals – Your goals can be useful in helping you move away from a lifestyle that does not suit you or move you toward the lifestyle you truly want. Mark Victor Hanson, author of the best selling book series *Chicken Soup for the Soul* believes that the goals that we extract from our values should be written down on 3x5 cards and looked at morning, noon, evening and before you go to bed. This process triggers your subconscious brain to take action in recreating your life.

4. Ask God for help in honoring your values, examing your motives, turning over the results to Him – James 4:3 in the Bible says, when you ask, you do not receive because you ask with the wrong motives (selfish motives). Looking deep within yourself prevents your values from becoming useless idols unto themselves.

5. Associate with folks who aren't afraid to tell you that you are "full of it" every once in a while – A professional growth coach, accountability partner or success team can be invaluable in letting you know not necessarily what you want to hear, but need to hear about the values you have been living.

Now, what I would like for you to do is to re-examine the following values on the following page that you prioritized in the earlier exercise. Take a moment and check off those three values that need to assume highest priority in your life right now. Then on the line next to the value, write down one action step that you are going to commit to in the next 30 days. Have someone follow-up with you during that period of time to ensure that you were true to yourself. If you don't have a person that will keep you accountable, call or E-mail us at Empowerment Unlimited Inc., (800) 804-0709, and we will call you!

VALUES AND COMMITMENTS

Michael Scott's Commitments	Your Commitments
❑ Romantic Life / Meaningful Relationships 1. Schedule a date night each week with Angie	❑ Romantic Life / Meaningful Relationships
❑ Spiritual Life 1. Read the Bible first thing in the morning 2. Pray Regularly	❑ Spiritual Life
❑ Personal Growth 1. Read at least 5 books each month	❑ Personal Growth
❑ Your Vocation 1. Write a book (Victory!)	❑ Your Vocation
❑ Family 1. Take 3 family vacations each year	❑ Family
❑ Health and Wellness 1. Drink more water (8 glasses a day) 2. Work six-hour work days 3. Take 1 healing day each month	❑ Health and Wellness
❑ Financial Situation 1. Set aside 10% of everything I earn and invest it in a mutual fund	❑ Financial Situation

LIFE DIRECTION KEY NO. 3 – UNLEASH YOUR VISION

All of us have dreams of things we want to do, places we want to go, people we want to meet that can bring richness to our lives. Your list might include vacationing in Palm Springs, playing golf in every state, or visiting Disney World and Epcot Center in Orlando. You may be a winter sports enthusiast who longs for a week of skiing in Vail, or a romantic getaway to the Pocono's, deep sea fishing in the Pacific, or a game of cricket in the Barbados. You may have a prompting to start your own business or take a year long sabbatical in a foreign country. Whatever your dreams, it is time to embrace them, celebrate them, plan for them. Dreams help to keep life engaging and fresh.

There is a friend of mine, Linda Cinkus, for whom I have a tremendous amount of admiration, because she had guts enough to embrace her dream! That dream involved moving to Phoenix from Chicago – alone – in order to be in an environment more conducive to her free spirit lifestyle. Recently I asked Linda whether the move was worth it and she said, "Without a doubt. I probably should have made this move years ago."

My wife and daughter are another example of two people embracing their vision. They find energy from their dream of visiting every Six Flags Great America theme park in the United States. My dream as I travel the country on speaking engagements is to visit every TGI Friday restaurant in the world. Note: With the speed in which TGI Fridays restaurants are being built, I expect to get to every one by the year 2027. Who cares if it takes me that long – I'm having fun!

When it comes to balance, always keep the following firmly implanted in your mind:

> *"True commitment to a balanced lifestyle begins with a vision! Burnout occurs when you lose sight of the vision! Rust-out occurs when you never had a vision!"*

Or, as the Bible verse goes, "Where there is no vision, people will perish."

Don't be among a growing number of individuals who are sleepwalking through a chaotic, pitiful, mediocre existence. Commit to pursuing your dreams. What you will find is that a lifestyle filled with future hopes creates the type of electricity which allows other parts of your life to fall in line.

PONDER AND ACT

Write down as many dreams as you possibly can in the box below. Why are these dreams important to you? Share them with supportive friends. Put a start date next to each one. Write down your thoughts and feelings in a journal as you engage in these activities.

DREAMS	START DATE

A LETTER SENT TO ME UNSOLICITED BY PAT McGLEAM OF McGLEAM PHOTOGRAPHY.

By the way, Pat's my photographer and does a superb job. Recently Pat's taken his life to another level because of several commitments he has made in the areas of life management.

Dear Michael:

I wanted to take a minute to thank you for the audio tape series *The Art Of Exceptional Living* by Jim Rohn. I listened to the six tapes last week and received invaluable insights and encouragement from them. Mr. Rohn is an excellent speaker and his enthusiasm is contagious. As an example, I rise about two hours earlier, walk two miles twice a day, joined a local church, and obtained a library card and use it regularly. I also placed an ad in three local papers touting a new digital retouch business that I have started. This is something I had put off for a long time. I am reading Steven Covey's *Seven Habits of Highly Effective People* and finding many similarities to Jim Rohn's tapes in the beginning chapters.

I had no idea of how to deal with what I felt was lacking in my life. Now I have a game plan starting with me. I am working on my list of goals. Last Thursday, I went shopping for an $85,000 car. There is no way that I can afford it now, but I wanted to see it, touch it, and sit in it to firmly place it in my mind as a goal for me for the future. I now have a picture of that car taped below my computer monitor, so that I see it every day as a reminder.

Thank you Michael, you helped me make a positive change in my life. Here's to our success.

Sincerely,

Patrick McGleam

Be like Pat. Embrace your dreams!

Part III
ACTION

Catch Your Balance And Run!

Chaos Management

> *The art of being wise is knowing what to overlook*
> – William James

We are often our own worst enemy when it comes to managing our time.

I'm sure you can relate to days when your life seems to veer out of control because you've created such unreasonable expectations around what you can accomplish in a 24-hour span of time. Then, if you're like me, you'll frequently beat yourself up at the end of the day over all those things that you were unable to get accomplished.

SO WHAT CAUSES OUR LIVES TO BE SO CHAOTIC?

Chaos, as I see it, often occurs because of one or more of the following traits:

- Perfection: When we attempt to structure our day without a degree of flexibility, we find ourselves stressed when the unexpected occurs.

- Excessive preoccupation with gaining the approval and avoiding the disapproval of others: Bill Cosby said it best when he remarked that, "I don't know the key to success, but the key to failure is trying to please everybody."

- Disorganization: A mere set of lost keys is often enough to throw a day into total pandemonium. In fact, studies estimate that we spend the equivalent of one year in our lifetime looking for misplaced objects!

- Interruptions: When we lose our focus it's more difficult to handle things in an efficient manner.

Before exploring ways in which to become be more effective time managers, I believe it's important for you to determine what are the three major factors that are impeding *your* ability to be more productive. Take a moment right now and write down the three factors that are impeding *your* daily productivity

1.
2.
3.

CHAOS MANAGEMENT KEYS

I believe there are six keys to maintaining integrity with yourself as you seek to reduce chaos and make more productive use of your time. Examine your responses above in line with the keys that follow:

1. GET REAL

If you've ever watched a team sporting event, chances are you've seen a game at some time or other where one of the teams gets woefully behind where it counts - on the scoreboard. They will often attempt to frantically catch up in the final minutes of the game only to fall short at the end. In fact, 9 times out of 10, in the midst of rushing to catch up, the team that is behind will often shoot themselves in the foot by making critical last minute mistakes, further compounding the pain of their defeat.

Do you find yourself rushing around at the very last minute to get things done? Ever lost something important like your car keys or glasses because you're in such a hurry? Experienced stress before as a result of trying to cram everything into a limited amount of time? If this sounds familiar, you may want to explore some ways in which to create a more realistic day. Here are just a few proven ideas that may be valuable to you as you strive to simultaneously *"CATCH YOUR BALANCE AND RUN."*

CHAOS REDUCTION IDEA #1 – Cluster routine activities: Studies tell us that you will make more effective use of your time if you schedule regular periods each week for activities such as writing bills, going to the bank, and taking shirts to the cleaners rather than flying by the seat of your pants.

CHAOS REDUCTION IDEA #2 – "List your priorities" rather than "prioritize a list": Many of us have "things to do lists" that are a mile long. Therefore, I believe it's more important to focus on those 5 - 7 items each day that truly make a difference rather than trying to prioritize a massive "things to do list" that even the greatest of time management experts couldn't conquer. For maximum effectiveness, prepare your list at the close of each day for the next day.

CHAOS REDUCTION IDEA #3 – Organize important items prior to going to bed: There is nothing that will get your day off to a worst start than to discover that you can't find your glasses, or that the suit and tie that you were planning to wear that day needs pressing. Or better yet, you are all showered and dressed, and on your way out of the door discover you can't locate your keys or your briefcase. People who are most effective in their use of time know that preparation the night before can be the difference between a successful versus disastrous start to the day.

CHAOS REDUCTION IDEA #4 – Plan your day realistically: A perfect example of this is when I'm about to fly out of town. To reduce the likelihood of having to rush frantically to my gate, I try to allow myself plenty of time for the unexpected – traffic, getting lost on the way to the airport if I'm out of town, heightened airport security, overbooked flights, and the potential of being bumped. I always arrive at an airport at least an hour early so I can move at a more measured pace and be able to anticipate any unexpected delays that might otherwise stress me out.

2. GET HELP

As the saying goes, "work smarter not harder." There are so many useful resources whose benefit more than exceeds the investment of money you will have to pay for them. If you find yourself trying to be all things to all people, all of the time, you may want to consider the following:

CLEANING SERVICE: There is nothing worse than having both a chaotic life and a messy house. Your investment in a cleaning service will be minuscule when you consider the time, energy and worry you will save from not having to handle the task yourself. Beyond a cleaning service, you may want to find a regular housekeeper who cooks! Wow! What a benefit!

FINANCIAL ADVISOR: If money management is a challenge for you, it's important to have trusted tax and money management advisors keep you on track.

BOOKKEEPER: If you have a small business or a rather complex tax situation, a good bookkeeper will save you tons of time and headaches! Personally, I simply toss all of my bank statements and receipts in a bag each month and send them off to my bookkeeper to have a ball with.

CHECK WRITER: You heard me right! There are actually individuals who specialize in paying and organizing your bills, and don't hyperventilate balancing your checkbook.

PERSONAL ASSISTANT: If you are among the growing ranks of small business owners, you will find it useful to have someone available to handle your correspondence, mailings, and other routine support activities. Burke Secretarial in Kansas City, Missouri, is the service I use and it has reduced the wear and tear on me associated with having to juggle these activities.

TRAVEL AGENT: If you travel a lot, a trusted travel advisor can be invaluable.

HOME HEALTH AIDE: Perhaps the most difficult decision my brother and I had to make when our Mother was fighting cancer was to solicit the assistance of a home health aide. Taking care of an ill relative is a challenge. If you are in a similar situation you will be well served by considering the benefits of this service. (Find out more about this in the following interview with Joy Loverde.)

• • • • • • • •

Interview With Joy Loverde On How To Balance The Needs Of Older Adult Parents With Our Other Time Demands

Joy Loverde, President of Silver Care Productions in Chicago, IL, is the nation's leading expert on elder care issues. She is the author of the best seller *The Elder Care Planner* which was published in partnership with the Disney Corporation.

Michael: Why is it that so many of us find ourselves unprepared to care for our aging parents? Why do we wait so long to plan for the inevitable?

Joy: The American family has undergone big changes. Family duties and tasks have changed. Nobody's home anymore. We're at work and at school. Complex lifestyles, time constraints and living greater distances from each other make it very challenging for family members to interact on a regular basis. Did you know that 75% of Americans watch television during meals? Simply put, important family conversations are no longer taking place around the dinner table.

Unfortunately, in our American culture, family members have been taught to wait for an eldercare crisis to occur and consequently, aren't even aware of what can happen unless they are currently experiencing an eldercare situation. None of us really know if and when a crisis may strike, when an issue will arise, or even know how to approach a parent about a "morbid" subject like funeral arrangements.

Yes, family eldercare issues are inevitable and thinking about the myriad needs of aging parents leaves most people overwhelmed, even immobilized. Also, talking about money, living arrangements, driving, and a host of other sensitive subjects with aging parents is not easy. And who wants to hash over unpleasant topics while Mom and Dad seem hale and healthy?

I don't meant to sound simplistic, but most families don't plan ahead because they don't know they can. My eldercare workshops are packed with people who say they wish that they had learned about my eldercare planning and communicating approach early on, avoiding unnecessary, serious problems – financially, emotionally and otherwise.

Physically being in the same room with our parents often wakes us up to the fact that they are aging. At first we notice subtle changes – walking slower, grappling for words. We may even uncover financial problems that we never knew existed. Something must be done, but what? Making astute observations and asking revealing questions are a few of my proven planning tips. Once family members become aware that it is possible to plan for inevitable family eldercare issues, they begin the process immediately.

Michael: What impact can taking care of an older adult parent have on our jobs? Our finances?

Joy: Eldercare is a complicated set of issues worsened by rising costs of care (skilled nursing care averages $105 per day, adult day care is $60 per day, home care averages $80 per visit), distance between loved ones (the majority of family members and their elders live at least 100 miles away from each other) and the extended family's assumptions of who will take on what responsibility when the time comes. And unlike childcare, eldercare can hit (and hit hard) an employee from out of nowhere, requiring immediate attention and an uncertain amount of time away from work plus an even more undetermined amount of time and attention over the long haul.

One out of every four employees is handling some level of family eldercare responsibilities. The process of locating eldercare resources, securing care services, talking on the telephone during office hours (much of which is long-distance), arguing with spouses and siblings over the details, partial and unplanned absenteeism (late arrivals, early departures, long lunch breaks) compounded by feelings of depression, anger, and guilt takes its toll on a company. Workday interruptions faced by employed family caregivers, are estimated at one hour per week per caregiver. This factor is the biggest drain of all on employee productivity. Family eldercare responsibilities require direct involvement and, lack of planning forces employees to be reactive, rather than proactive, too often resulting in hasty and costly decisions. The disruption at work (and at home) is significant.

Michael: Joy, I recall how difficult a decision it was for my brother and me in deciding whether to place Mom in an extended care facility when she was ill. Any advise for those confronted with a similar situation?

Joy: Michael, the advice I have to share regarding this sensitive issue lies in your phrase, "when she was ill." Inevitable transitions in an aging person's lifestyle – retirement, chronic illness, repositioning of finances, limited mobility – signal that it is time for the family to examine their elder's current and future housing and care needs.

Contrary to popular belief, most of the elderly are not ill. Only six percent of people over the age of 65 require skilled nursing home care. The majority of the aging population live independently - in spite of their aches and pains - with the help of family, friends and community outreach programs. Study after study indicates that most elderly people want to remain in their own homes and communities, but lack of proper planning often forces them to live otherwise. To assume that nursing home care will be an inevitable eldercare issue is outdated thinking. Unless an elderly person requires 24-hour supervision and extensive health care assistance, there are many other housing and care choices available.

On the other hand, family members may be reluctant to consider an extended care facility when they should. The time may come when we can't do it all or don't have the resources to give our aging relative the proper care required. Yes, the decision to place an elder in an extended care facility is a difficult one, but sometimes it is the only alternative. It is not a question of whether or not institutionalized care is inherently good or bad. The decision for this option should be based on health care needs, preference of the family caregiver, finances, and the availability of quality facilities. The choice is a very personal one. During these times, open communication and planning ahead are vital, emphasizing the importance of making decisions that work to the benefit of the entire family.

Michael: Tell us about *The Complete Eldercare Planner* that you authored.

Joy: Because the true nature of assisting an aging family member includes a roller coaster of emotional upsets, the process of family caregiving requires nothing less than a consistent management of attitudes, choices and plans. Perhaps the hardest part of eldercare is when family members ask themselves, "Am I doing the right thing?" To feel as if we are effectively staying on top of the medical, financial and personal issues associated with eldercare, today's busy family caregivers benefit from my book which condenses the long hours of experience and research into plans of action.

The Complete Eldercare Planner is the roadmap through unfamiliar, emotional and complex eldercare territory. Written with the time-taxed reader in mind, this specialty-designed resource offers manageable, step-by-step action plans for real-life eldercare problems like emergency preparedness, how to tell when a parent needs help, talking about sensitive subjects, sharing the care, housing, long-distance assistance, money and legal matters, and insurance for a longer life.

The Complete Eldercare Planner is also the first guide to offer in the same book low-cost, free resources, a Website index, questions to ask with places to write down answers, space to record elder's vital medical, financial and personal information, and checklists to keep readers on track. Effective planning is specific, realistic and written.

Eldercare equals planning for our family's future. Talking with Mom and Dad now, while they are healthy and hearty, is the best time to initiate eldercare conversations. This way, employees and their aging parents can open up the dialogue and proactively address the difficult questions together – what can happen and what can we do about what happens - before issues reach crisis mode.

Employees who are just starting to think about eldercare issues are wise to review The Cost of Caring chapter in my book. The taboo regarding talking about money with our parents has been lifted. Due to a longer life expectancy, most of today's elders will outlive their money and when the money runs out, the rest of the family typically picks up the tab.

As if assisting aging parents with the basics of living isn't stressful enough, we family members are also expected to have access to important and legal information and documents. At any given time, we are expected to have knowledge of insurance policies, medical histories, income tax returns, medications, property titles, social security numbers, names and telephone numbers of doctors, and more. The paperwork is overwhelming. The worse case scenario is trying to get answers under emergency conditions. What if our parents are too sick to advise us of any answers or, arrangements have not been made ahead of time to perform legal and financial transactions on their behalf? The good news is *The Complete Eldercare Planner* has an extensive Documents Locator and readers can get started on eldercare paperwork immediately.

As you can see, it is possible for family members to plan ahead, and doing so offers continued productivity at work, peace of mind, plus a quality of life for generations to come.

● ● ● ● ● ● ●

3. GET FOCUSED

One of the major reasons we often find our lives so chaotic is because we fail to slow down and take the necessary time to focus our activities. In his best selling book *Flow: The Psychology of Optimal Experience,* the author, Mihaly Csikszentmihalyi discusses his findings on states of "optional experience" – those situations when people report feelings of deep focus, concentration, and deep enjoyment. This author believes that these pleasurable states can, in fact, be controlled by establishing goals that are neither too difficult nor too simple for our abilities.

My belief is that many of us end up being less than productive in our efforts because we either "overload or underload" our schedule. In other words, true focus and productivity occur when you concentrate on those few important things first, versus a long list of items that upon examination you find are not all that important.

Here are a couple of easy to implement ideas to experiment with in your efforts to become more focused:

A. Find a quite place to reflect: It's important that we take the time on a regular basis to allow for quiet reflection. Retreat to a quiet chapel or even your kitchen table early in the morning and get your thoughts in order. This allows you to slow down your internal dialogue with yourself and become focused rather than scattered in your activities. Note: The book, *The Seven Spiritual Laws of Success* by Deepak Chopra is an excellent guide for helping you tap into this valuable source of focus.

B. Practice focusing on one thing at a time: Years ago, I asked a very wise man what his secrets of success were relative to time management. His response was rather profound yet simple. He said, "you must eliminate distractions and focus on one thing at a time."

As you look at your daily endeavors, ask yourself the questions, "what distractions are preventing me from reaching my highest level of productivity? What can I do to eliminate them in order to become more focused?"

As I explored these questions in my own life, it became readily apparent that there was one major distraction that was hindering me from becoming all that I wanted to be professionally – the phone. Often when I was in my office working on a major project, someone would call and interrupt my concentration. Often it was a call that could have been handled at a later date or by my National Meetings Director.

After unsuccessfully trying to allow the phone to ring without answering it, which drove me next to nuts, a friend of mine suggested that I might want to turn the ringer off during those peak periods of intense concentration. What a huge difference this one simple suggestion made in what I'm able to accomplish on any given day!

QUICKIE EXERCISE

Identify three ongoing distractions for you at work or home. Discuss with a trusted friend or success partner what works for them with regards to handling the distractions. Take each of these new ways of managing the distractions and try them for 31 days. Ask your friend or partner to follow up with you regularly to see if you're remaining accountable to yourself.

DISTRACTIONS	**WAYS OF MANAGING IT**
_____	_____
_____	_____
_____	_____
_____	_____

4. GET RENEWED

My prediction is that those who are most successful in managing their time commitments will be those individuals who work fewer hours than the norm. While studies, such as the ones produced by the Work and Family Institute tell us that the average workweek continues to increase, there appears to be a segment of the population moving away from the 60-plus hour grind and more towards a lifestyle of renewal and refocus.

5. GET AWAY!

That's right. Get away from saying yes to others and commitments that don't serve you. It's not until you say <u>no</u> to the unimportant that you are able to say <u>yes</u> to the important.

The Bible provides us with a wonderful story about an individual who had great difficulty in saying no. His name was Moses. In the book of Exodus Chapter 18, it was said that Moses, as leader of the Israelites, was surrounded by an endless number of requests for decisions by the people . . . thousands of people. It was further reported that Moses literally sat to judge the people from morning to evening. . .the classic account of an ancient workaholic! Finally his wise father-in-law (Jethro) challenged his "let me be all things to all people" philosophy by asking him, "Why do you alone sit as judge and all the people stand about you from morning to evening?" Then he tells Moses, "This thing that you are doing is not good. You will surely wear out both yourself and the people who are with you, for the task is too heavy for you. You cannot do it alone." Heeding his father-in-law's advice, Moses made the wise choice to divide up his responsibility among his trusted leaders.

Can you relate to Moses? We would all probably agree that it's hard to say no to others, particularly when it may be tied to what they may think about us, or our job security.

6. GET PEPPY!

PEP stands for Peak Energy Periods. We all have them and it's imperative that we use them to our advantage.

QUICKIE EXERCISE

Take a moment and think about whether you are a morning, afternoon, or evening person. List your five most important activities for tomorrow under the period when your energy is highest and if possible focus on those activities during that peak time period. Explore whether making this shift makes a difference, and continue doing it if it does.

MY HIGH ENERGY PERIOD

MORNING	AFTERNOON	EVENING
1.		
2.		
3.		
4.		
5.		

Attitude Management

> *Your attitude determines your altitude!*

Attitude! Countless self-help books have been written about it. Quotes about having a "positive attitude" have motivated many to greatness. Some say that attitude is the "ultimate aphrodisiac." Others call it "the perpetual downer." So what is attitude and how does it relate to balance? Like it or not – and often we don't – attitude determines whether we live a life of chaos or a life of contentment; a life where we stand tall and be counted or a life where we get knocked down and counted out; a life of moaning or a life of meaning.

There is nothing revolutionary about the following observations about attitude. They amount to reflections on my 34 years of life, and making adjustments along the often unpredictable journey of life!

1. Maintain a Sense of Humor

By keeping life lighthearted and fun you'll be able to keep life in it's proper perspective even in the midst of challenging times. Looking for a real jolt on how to maintain a sense of humor as you balance work, family and other priorities? I encourage you to pick up a book entitled *Nuts! The Southwest Airlines Story* by Frieberg and Frieberg. This book exposes you to the "have fun at all costs" philosophy that has allowed Southwest to become the only domestic airline that has made a profit every year of its existence. Their employees don't believe in the chronic seriousness that is common among other airlines. They utilize humor to keep the customers as well as fellow employees in step with what is truly important. Flight attendants, in fact, have been known to sing to on-board passengers over the public address system, lay sideways in overhead luggage compartments, and use their own favorite version of FAA passenger regulations that are both informative and silly.

You're probably saying to yourself at this point, "I don't have a sense of humor." Wrong! We all have the capacity to be humorous, particularly when it comes to opening up about those embarrassing moments in our lives. And just when we're struggling to find something in life to laugh about, God finds a way to make us look at life a bit differently.

For example, at my Mother's funeral in 1993, something unusual happened to my brother that helped to loosen us all up. We were leaving the cemetery in the limo with the immediate family. I looked out the back rear window only to see my brother, David, frantically chasing the limo. In the midst of all of our grief and ceremony we almost left David at the gravesite! What a humorous thing to have happen in the midst of such a difficult day for all of us.

2. Break Up Recurring Patterns

Many of us suffer through such unsatisfying lives because our movie script is the same everyday. We get up, get the kids dressed, take them to school, drive to work, pick them up, go home, eat dinner, watch TV, and then go to sleep.

Those of us who live healthy, fulfilled and balanced lives know that a bit of variety every now and then is key. We know that variety keeps us on our toes and aware of what is happening around us. In fact, because our days are so regimented, we often realize that we've placed ourselves in a potentially harmful or compromising position. For example, I bet at some point within the last six months you have driven home from work, totally oblivious to what is happening around you, only to discover that you didn't even remember the drive home! Maybe this experience is telling you that a new route is in order.

> *Do not use a hatchet to remove a fly from a friends forehead.* – Chinese Proverb

3. Listen To Others With Love

Our selfish attitudes towards others can create chaos and unbalance in our lives because of the conflict it often creates. There is perhaps no better route to creating loving, meaningful relationships with others than to be a good listener, for it is often said that "the greatest need of another human being is the need to be heard."

Recently, I was in a shopping mall in Columbus, Ohio, quietly reading a book when I began to overhear a heated discussion between a couple regarding some work/family conflicts they were facing. What was so sad about this discussion was the fact that neither person was hearing the other. They were both so intent on verbally blaming each other for the difficulties they were facing that nothing appeared to have been resolved after nearly an hour and a half.

If this sounds familiar, I encourage you to spend more time listening to your loved ones. I know from experience how powerful the process of empathy and understanding can be in resolving many conflicts.

Note: By now you've probably guessed that I am a bookaholic. Many would say that I acquired this chronic illness from my Dad who was an avid reader as well. Because I, like you, continually seek ways to create more meaningful relationships with others, again allow me to recommend a book that I guarantee will make a difference in resolving relationship based conflicts. It is called *The Heart of Conflict* by Brian Muldoon. Pick it up today!

4. Avoid Energy Drainers

Let's face it, some people make it their personal business and lifelong purpose to create disharmony in our lives. Recently, a friend of mine was telling me about the people she had to weed out of her life because they were just that – weeds. They were constantly calling and moaning about their spouses, about how life has dealt them a bad hand of cards, about not having any money to do anything. She said, "Michael, they were draining me of the energy I need in order to ensure that my own life is in order."

Sometimes a good vacuuming is necessary in order to allow some clarity in your life. Don't hesitate to clean house every once in a while and replace toxic folks with some good furniture.

5. Opt for O-P-T

Did you know that you can literally change the direction of your life by only allowing positive, affirming thoughts in your mind? It's a process I referred to as OPT which stands for Only Positive Thoughts. You see, negative thoughts which are firmly rooted in your mind are like cancer – they spread quickly and are hard to remove.

My life and the way I view the complexities of today's fast-paced world changed dramatically when I stopped allowing negative, self-depreciating thoughts to rule me. Whenever I see a negative thought headed up the highway toward the frontal lobe of my brain, I simply say to myself – "OPT, negative thoughts are not allowed!" And then just like operating a TV remote control, I immediately change the channel. Or I will replace the negative thought with a positive one.

> *As a man thinketh, so is he* – Proverbs 23:7

6. Connect With the Spiritual Synchronicities of Life

A big part of your attitude about life centers around how well you're willing to accept those daily meaningful occurrences that are a part of God's divine plan. As Jesus says to his Father in Matthew 26:39, "Not as I will but as you will."

Synchronicity calls you to be consciously aware of those meaningful occurrences in your life. It calls you to view everything in life as ultimately good because when you really think about it, bad is just simply a state of mind. Approach every day as though it were your last and you want to be remembered for it. Spiritual Synchronicity says, fear not because as the Lord your God, everything I will is perfect. Celebrate now and expect great things to happen as you continuously *CATCH YOUR BALANCE AND RUN!*

Catch Your Balance And Run!

Afterword
•••••••
To Do's: A Baker's Dozen

You may be asking yourself at this point, "But what, among this mass of ideas, should be my priorities?" I can't really answer that, but, opinionated as I am, I couldn't resist trying.

1. Firmly establish your personal definition of life balance. During the next 30 days, review your definition with at least 10 friends or family members. Then, make a formal pledge to yourself, or at least commit to trying it on for size for a month.

2. Acknowledge your life balance challenges. Doing this is nine-tenths of the battle relative to creating a more meaningful lifestyle.

3. Determine what values are taking up most of your time, energy and attention currently. Discuss with friends and family. Launch initiatives in line with your desired values.

4. Nurture what you perceive to be your purpose or calling. Work with a personal/professional coach or counselor to get clearer as to what this may be and how it fits in with your other life priorities.

5. Put together a dream list of 100+ things you've always wanted to do. Take action on at least two each month. Celebrate each victory!

6. Detach yourself from trying to be "all things to all people." Start today by concentrating on being present in the moment – acknowledging that God has you right where he wants you to be at this very moment.

7. Examine your priorities and choices and begin to ask yourself, "What really is most important? If I passed away today, would the things I accomplished make that big of a difference."

8. Practice focusing on one important thing at a time (Note: This may be the greatest time management tool ever invented. And, you won't spend half your life looking for lost items. Promise!)

9. Stop and smell the roses ever so often. There is a lot of wisdom in the statement, "All work and no play makes Jack and Jackie dull people" – and burned out people at that!

10. Maintain a sense of humor. Laugh often, tell bad jokes, do anything to avoid chronic seriousness.

11. Excrete toxic thoughts from our system. Excuse yourself from the company of toxic folks.

12. Have faith, trust in God, and enjoy your life as it unfolds.

Good Luck!

Mike

MICHAEL SCOTT EMPOWERMENT UNLIMITED INC.
● ● ● ● ● ● ●

List of Recommended Books

THE BIBLE. The Bible, clearly stands above all other books as the authoritative source for life. *(The Life Application Bible – New Revised Standard Version*, Tyndale House Publishers, Inc., is my personal favorite.)

THE 7 HABITS OF HIGHLY EFFECTIVE PEOPLE. Stephen Covey, Simon and Shuster, Inc., 1989, ISBN 0-671-66398-4 (Perhaps the finest book that I have ever read outside of the Bible.)

THE COMPLETE ELDERCARE PLANNER. Joy Loverde, Hyperion Publishers, New York, NY, ISBN 0-7868-8229-8 (An absolute must if managing the needs of an older adult parent.)

THE PURSUIT OF WOW!. Tom Peters, Vintage Books, ISBN 0-679-75555-1 (A humorous yet practical guide to life. You've got to be a little crazy to read this one!)

THE FIVE RITUALS OF WEALTH. Todd Barnhart, Harper Collins Publishers, 1996 ISBN 0-88730-784-1 (An excellent how-to guide to achieving and maintaining wealth. Especially useful if you feel like you never have enough money.)

NUTS!. Kevin & Jackie Freiberg, Bard Press Inc., 1996, ISBN 1-885167-18-0 (The Southwest Airlines success story. Great for leaders who desire a highly productive work environment that's fun!)

TIME TACTICS OF VERY SUCCESSFUL PEOPLE. B. Eugene Griessman, McGraw Hill Inc., 1994, ISBN 0-07-024644-0 (If managing your time is a struggle, you need this book!)

ORGANIZING FOR THE CREATIVE PERSON. Dorothy Lehmkuhl and Dolores Lamping, Crown Trade Paperbacks, New York, NY, 1993, ISBN 0-517-88164-0 (A must if you find getting organized painful.)

NO MAN IS AN ISLAND. Thomas Merton, Harcourt Brace and Company, New York, NY, 1955, ISBN 0-15-665962-X (Searching for the meaning of life? This book will provide you with some unique spiritual/philosophical perspectives to mull over.)

FLOW: THE PSYCHOLOGY OF OPTIMAL EXPERIENCE. Mihaly Csikszentmihalyi, Harper Collins Publishers, New York, NY, 1990, ISBN 0-06-092043-2 (Life will take on a whole new meaning after reading this one!)

AHA! 10 WAYS TO FREE YOUR CREATIVE SPIRIT AND FIND YOUR GREAT IDEAS. Jordan Ayan, Crown Publishing Group, New York, NY, 1997, ISBN 0-517-88400-3 (This book stimulated more ideas than I could possibly implement in a lifetime!)

RADICAL HONESTY: HOW TO TRANSFORM YOUR LIFE BY TELLING THE TRUTH. Brad Blanton, Ph.D., Dell Publishing, New York, NY, 1996, ISBN 0-440-50754-5 (Don't read this book unless you're ready to stop lying to others as well as yourself!)

TIME MANAGEMENT FOR UNMANAGEABLE PEOPLE. Ann McGee-Cooper, Duane Trammell, Bantam Doubleday Dell Publishing, New York, NY, 1994, ISBN 0-553370715 (This book provides fun and very practical tips for managing your time effectively.)

YOU DON'T HAVE TO GO HOME FROM WORK EXHAUSTED: A PROGRAM TO BRING JOY, ENERGY AND BALANCE TO YOUR LIFE. Ann McGee-Cooper, Duane Trammel, Bantam Doubleday Dell Publishing, New York, NY, 1982, ISBN 0-553370618 (One of the best books on renewal I've read in years!)

IF YOU WEAR OUT YOUR BODY, WHERE WILL YOU LIVE? Barb Schwarz Book Partners, Inc., Wilsonville, Oregon, ISBN 1-885221-66-5 (Looking to rejuvenate your body, mind and soul through nutritional choices and a plan for your personal potential? Then this book is for you!)

I'M TOO BLESSED TO BE DEPRESSED: STORIES TO MOVE YOU FROM STRESSED TO BLESSED. Joanna Slan, Chesterfield, MO (This powerful book of stories will reinvigorate you and remind you that you are truly blessed.)

CALLINGS: FINDING AND FOLLOWING AN AUTHENTIC LIFE. Gregg Levoy, Crown Publishers, New York, NY, ISBN 0-5177056-9-9 (Lost as to what your calling is? This book provides some excellent insights into recognizing the turning points in your life and what they mean.)

THE HEART OF CONFLICT. Brian Muldoon, Putnam Publishing Group, New York, NY, ISBN 0-3991418-0-4 (Outstanding practical resource for handling conflicts both at work and at home.)

Visit our website at www.power2u.com and order your books via our internet bookstore! You'll save money and receive your order in 2-3 days.

Catch Your Balance And Run!

ABOUT THE AUTOR
MICHAEL SCOTT
● ● ● ● ● ● ●

Michael Scott is the President of Empowerment Unlimited Inc., a South Bend, Indiana based firm dedicated to working with individuals who want to maximize their untapped potential and organizations that want to reach that next level of success. Michael has an extensive background as a business executive and is a highly regarded keynote presenter, seminar leader and business advisor. He conducts over 100 presentations each year for groups ranging from Fortune 500 companies, to trade associations nationwide. Michael's extensive list of clients include National Institutes of Health, IBM, Texas Instruments, and the American Society of Association Executives just to name a few. His background includes sound academics as well as successful life experiences through the "University of Hard Knocks." His articles have appeared in numerous national and international publications including *Personal Excellence*, a Franklin/Covey organization publication. Michael is a member of the National Speakers Association.